indoor grilling

indoor grilling

hamlyn

Notes

The American Egg Board advises that eggs should not be consumed raw. This book contains some dishes made with raw or lightly cooked eggs. It is prudent for more vulnerable people such as pregnant and nursing mothers, invalids, the elderly, babies, and young children to avoid uncooked or lightly cooked dishes made with eggs.

Meat and poultry should be cooked thoroughly. To test if poultry is cooked, pierce the flesh through the thickest part with a skewer or fork – the juices should run clear, never pink or red. Keep refrigerated until ready for cooking.

This book includes dishes made with nuts and nut derivatives. It is advisable for those with known allergic reactions to nuts and nut derivatives and those who may potentially be vulnerable to these allergies, such as pregnant and nursing mothers, invalids, the elderly, babies, and children, to avoid dishes made with nuts and nut oils. It is also prudent to check the labels of pre-prepared ingredients for the possible inclusion of nut derivatives.

First published in Great Britain in 2004 by Hamlyn,
a division of Octopus Publishing Group Ltd,
2–4 Heron Quays, London E14 4JP

ISBN 0 600 61247 3

A CIP catalog record for this book is available from the British Library

Printed and bound in China
10 9 8 7 6 5 4 3 2 1

contents

introduction

Indoor grilling is a convenient and increasingly popular cooking method. As the range of grill pans and indoor grills increases, more and more people are discovering indoor grilling and recognizing the health benefits and full-on flavor of grilled food.

This is a very versatile way to cook—the range of ingredients and dishes that can be grilled is enormous. From steaks and sausages to sizzling shrimp and fish, from Mediterranean vegetables to chunks of rum-soaked pineapple, grilled foods are tempting and tasty.

the health benefits of grilling

Apart from the wonderful flavor of the food, the main benefit of indoor grilling is that you do not need to add any extra fat or oil during cooking. Most of us would benefit from reducing our fat intake, and indoor grilling can help you do just that. Some people prefer to brush or spray cast-iron grill pans with a little oil when cooking more delicate foods such as vegetables and shrimp, but if the pan is heated sufficiently before adding the food, this is not necessary.

choosing a grill pan

Stove-top grill pans Stove-top grill pans can be round or square in shape and often have a spout on one side for pouring off juices or excess fat from the food. They are usually heavier than normal pans because they must withstand very high temperatures.

There are nonstick and cast-iron pans available. As the name suggests, food is less likely to stick to a nonstick pan, but sticking should not be a problem if a cast-iron pan is heated sufficiently before use. Cast-iron pans will last forever because there is no coating to be damaged, but they are heavy and can be difficult to manage.

Most grill pans have a ridged surface so the food is held above any fat that runs out of it. Grill pans with a flat surface are often referred to as griddles. These are used for cooking pancakes and patties but they can be used for other foods too. Choose the heaviest pan you can afford as this will ensure quality.

Electric grills The best electric indoor grills have heated bars on which the food is cooked. This allows the food to be close to the heat source and cook evenly. The cooking surface is usually nonstick for easy cooking and cleaning. The fat drops beneath the bars and is collected in a tray for disposal. The recipes in this book are designed with a stove-top grill pan in mind, but they can also be cooked on an electric grill.

tips for successful grilling

- Read the manufacturer's guidelines before using your grill pan. They are all slightly different.
- The pan should be hot when the food is added. Heat the empty pan over medium heat for 5–10 minutes. The time it needs depends on the type of pan—cast-iron will take longer to come up to temperature.
- There is usually no need to add any oil or fat when cooking in a grill pan. Sausages and other fatty meats certainly won't need any, but you can oil the pan lightly when cooking fish, shrimp, or vegetables.
- Adjust the temperature so foods cook quickly but do not burn. If the temperature is too low, juices will run out of the food and it will steam rather than grill. If the temperature is too high, the food will burn on the outside before the inside is cooked. Experience will help you achieve the right temperature.

- Do not turn the food until it has had time to form a golden crust underneath (check this by carefully lifting it with a spatula) to keep the juices sealed in. Then turn it over and allow a crust to form on the other side.
- Turn down the temperature when the food is sealed on all sides to allow it to cook through without burning.
- Cook food according to your liking. Sausages, pork, and poultry must be cooked through. Test by inserting the tip of a sharp knife or a skewer into the thickest part—the juices should run clear. If they are at all pink, continue to cook. Beef and lamb can be served pink inside.
- The pan can be deglazed once the food has been cooked to make a flavorful sauce. Add a little wine, brandy, stock, or cream to the pan to mix with the pan juices, season with salt and pepper to taste, and cook until you achieve the desired consistency.

caring for your pan

Read the manufacturer's instructions on how best to care for your pan. Always use wooden utensils with nonstick pans to avoid damaging the coating. Allow the pan to cool completely before attempting to clean it. Nonstick pans should be washed in warm soapy water with a soft cloth and then dried thoroughly. Avoid using scourers or abrasive cleaning products.

Cast-iron pans should be filled with warm soapy water immediately after use to make them easier to clean when they have become cool.

flavoring grilled foods

The goal of indoor grilling is to use the best possible ingredients, which need little embellishment to make them delicious. Because the process imparts so much flavor, simple grilled meats, vegetables, and fish are wonderful as they are. However, grilled foods need not be plain—there are many different flavoring ingredients that will add a little excitement. This book presents a delicious collection of recipes featuring a wide range of wonderful ingredients. Try Grilled Italian Lamb with Rosemary Oil, or Cajun Blackened Chicken with Avocado Salad. If you like seafood, then Grilled Bream with Ginger and Shallots, or Lime, Coconut and Chili-Spiked Squid are for you. Or what about Spicy Zucchini Fritters, or Grilled Thyme-Marinated Goat's Milk Cheeses? There are a range of grilled desserts as well, including Grilled Panettone with Peaches and Cream, and Grilled Pineapple with Rum and Mascarpone. Or try using some of the flavoring ingredients listed below to transform your grilled foods.

Herbs Fresh herbs add zing to just about any grilled foods. Use them generously to enjoy their individual flavors to the fullest. Add delicate leafy herbs, such as parsley, mint, and basil, toward the end of cooking so they are not burned. Woody herbs, such as rosemary and thyme, are more robust and can be added earlier in the cooking process to impart greater flavor to the food. Try mint or tarragon with

chicken, shrimp, or lamb; basil or parsley with fish or vegetables; sage with pork or chicken; and rosemary and thyme with red meats, duck, or vegetables.

fresh aromatics

• Garlic is invaluable when grilling and enhances just about any meat, fish, or vegetables. Use it in marinades and herb butters, or add crushed or chopped garlic to the pan toward the end of the cooking time to prevent it from burning. Continue to cook until the garlic is soft and lightly golden.
• Ginger adds a spicy aromatic note to grilled foods and is most popular in Asian dishes. Add finely chopped or sliced fresh ginger to marinades or sprinkle it over grilling meats, fish, or vegetables.

- Lemongrass is another Asian ingredient, and it provides a fresh zestiness. Chop finely and sprinkle over meat and poultry as they cook, or use with chopped garlic and chilies to make a coating for chicken breasts and pork tenderloin. Lemongrass is also surprisingly good with steaks.
- Chilies can be used fresh and finely chopped, as dried flakes, as a powder, or can be served whole for garnishing. They add piquancy and heat to any savory dish, but don't add them to the grill too soon or the juicy flesh will burn and lose its taste. Add as much or as little as you like but remember that the smaller, thinner chilies are the hottest. Remove the seeds if you don't like your food too hot.

Flavored oils and butters Savory oils and butters, flavored with herbs, spices, and other aromatics are great for drizzling or melting over grilled meat and fish after cooking. Experiment with different combinations to achieve different tastes.

To make an herb butter, finely chop some fresh herbs, chilies, or ginger, and mash with butter and a little crushed garlic. Place the mixture on a square of wax paper, form into a log shape, wrap tightly and refrigerate until you are ready to eat. Serve the grilled food with a slice of herb butter on top.

There are two ways to make an herb oil. One way is to add some chopped fresh herbs and aromatics to a little olive oil, season to taste and drizzle it over your grilled food. The other is to add whole chilies, sprigs of rosemary or thyme, and garlic cloves to a bottle of olive oil and leave it to marinate for a few days, shaking it from time to time. Then pass the mixture through a strainer to remove the other ingredients and leave just the flavored oil. Use for drizzling as above.

Spices Whole or ground spices can also transform a plain piece of meat or fish. Try cumin seeds, coriander, crushed juniper berries, ground cayenne, or paprika to add warm, deep flavors. Chili powder and ground black pepper are also invaluable ingredients to add a spicy note.

making a sauce

Although it may sound unlikely, indoor grilling is a great way to produce a delicious sauce with your meal. You will need to use a stove-top grill pan for this. When your meat or fish is cooked through, add a little stock, wine, or brandy to the pan and allow it to bubble until well reduced. It will mingle with the cooking juices from the meat or fish and make a wonderful sauce. The reducing time will vary depending on the amount of liquid, so keep an eye on the pan. If necessary skim off any froth on the surface. Once reduced, season the sauce with salt and pepper. Add a little yogurt, sour cream, or cream if you prefer a richer sauce. Above all, feel free to experiment to produce a range of exciting dishes.

appetizers, salads, and vegetables

grilled vegetable soup

1 red onion, sliced into flat pieces
4 red bell peppers, cored, seeded, and
cut into flat pieces
2 zucchini, sliced
1 eggplant, sliced
2 garlic cloves, sliced
1 3/4 cups organic tomato juice
1/3 cup freshly grated Parmesan
cheese
1 bunch basil, chopped
1/3 cup olive oil
sea salt and black pepper
bread, to serve

Serves 4
Preparation time 15 minutes
Cooking time 35–40 minutes

This is a delicious, healthy soup, full of the flavor of fresh vegetables. It makes a perfect appetizer in summer.

1 Heat a grill pan over a medium heat. First grill all the vegetables in batches, then set aside. Grill the onion slices for 5 minutes on each side. Grill the pepper pieces for 6 minutes on the skin side only, until charred and blistered, and peel away the charred skin when the peppers are cool enough to handle. Grill the zucchini slices for 4 minutes on each side, the eggplant slices for 5 minutes on each side, and the garlic slices for 1 minute on each side.

2 Place all the grilled vegetables in a food processor or blender, reserving a few zucchini slices for garnish, add the tomato juice, and process roughly for a soup with a little texture or process until smooth, according to your preference.

3 Place the grated Parmesan in a small bowl. Add the chopped basil, olive oil, and a little salt and pepper, and mix well.

4 Check the soup and add salt and pepper to taste. Serve it hot or cold with bread and garnished with the reserved zucchini slices and a little of the Parmesan and basil mixture. Serve the remainder separately at the table for guests to help themselves.

new potato and green onion cakes

1 lb new potatoes
4 green onions, finely sliced
1 egg, lightly beaten
1 tablespoon olive oil
1 tablespoon chopped parsley
1 tablespoon chopped chives
2 teaspoons wholegrain mustard
1 teaspoon paprika
sea salt and black pepper
green onions or chives, to garnish

Sour cream dressing
1 cup sour cream
2 tablespoons chopped chives
1 tablespoon lemon juice
freshly cracked black pepper

Serves 4
Preparation time 10 minutes
Cooking time 25–30 minutes

1 Bring a pan of salted water to a boil and cook the potatoes for 10–12 minutes until cooked but firm. Drain, then return to the pan and allow to cool.

2 Meanwhile, make the sour cream dressing, mix together all the ingredients and season to taste with black pepper.

3 When the potatoes are cool, add the green onions, egg, olive oil, parsley, chives, mustard, and paprika to the pan, and crush the potatoes with the back of a fork until they are broken up but not mashed. Season well with salt and pepper.

4 Heat a grill pan over a medium heat. Place 3-inch round cutters on a baking pan and fill with the potato mixture, pushing it down gently so that the cakes do not fall apart. Using a metal spatula, gently lift the potato-filled cutters onto the heated grill pan and cook for 3–4 minutes. When golden, gently remove the cutters and carefully flip the cakes over and cook for an additional 3–4 minutes until crisp and golden. Keep the potato cakes warm while you cook the remaining potato mixture. You should be able to make 8 cakes in all.

5 To serve, place 2 crushed potato cakes on each plate with a spoonful of sour cream dressing and sprinkle with green onions or chives.

parmesan and herb polenta wedges with tomato salsa

2/3 cup instant polenta or cornmeal

2 cups simmering water

6 tablespoons (3/4 stick) butter

1/2 cup freshly grated Parmesan
  cheese

2 tablespoons chopped chives

2 tablespoons roughly chopped parsley

2 tablespoons chopped chervil

sea salt and black pepper

Spicy cherry tomato salsa

10 oz ripe cherry tomatoes, quartered

2 small red chilies, seeded
  and finely chopped

1 small red onion, finely chopped

2 tablespoons chili oil

2 tablespoons olive oil

2 tablespoons lime juice

2 tablespoons shredded mint

Serves 4
Preparation time 10 minutes
Cooking time 15–20 minutes

1 Pour the polenta into a pan of simmering water and beat well with a wooden spoon until it is thick and smooth. Reduce the heat and continue stirring for about 5 minutes (or according to the package instructions) to cook the polenta.

2 Remove the pan from the heat and add the butter, Parmesan, chives, parsley, and chervil and stir until well combined. Season with salt and pepper then turn into a greased 10-inch pizza or cake pan, at least 1 inch deep. Smooth the top with the back of a spoon and let set for about 5–10 minutes.

3 Combine all the salsa ingredients in a bowl and season with salt and pepper to taste. Set aside.

4 Carefully remove the set polenta from the pan, transfer it to a cutting board, and cut into 8 wedges.

5 Heat a grill pan over a high heat. Place the polenta wedges on the grill pan and cook for 2–3 minutes on each side, until heated through and golden. Serve 2 wedges to each person with a spoonful of the salsa on the side.

beet, feta, and treviso salad

1 lb raw beets, peeled and cut into
   1/2-inch slices
1 large head or 1 cup treviso
2 tablespoons extra virgin olive oil
1 tablespoon red wine vinegar
1 bunch flat-leaf parsley, chopped
8 oz feta cheese, to garnish
sea salt and black pepper

Serves 4
Preparation time 10 minutes
Cooking time 12 minutes

Treviso is a member of the chicory family, with a slightly bitter taste. If you cannot find any, use Belgian endive or arugula instead.

1 Heat a grill pan over a medium heat. Put the beet slices on the grill and cook on each side for 4–5 minutes. Transfer to a mixing bowl.

2 Cut the treviso into wedges and remove the hard core. Place the treviso on the grill and cook until just wilted, then add to the beets.

3 Add the olive oil, vinegar, and chopped parsley to the beets and treviso. Season with salt and pepper to taste and toss well. Transfer to a serving dish, crumble the feta over the top, and serve.

fennel and butter bean salad

1 fennel bulb
2 green bell peppers, quartered, cored, and seeded
1 8-oz can butter beans, drained and rinsed well
3 1/2 oz feta cheese
3 tablespoons pine nuts, toasted
1 bunch parsley, chopped, plus extra to garnish
5 tablespoons olive oil
sea salt and black pepper

Serves 4
Preparation time 10 minutes
Cooking time 15 minutes

1 Heat a grill pan over a medium heat. Thinly slice the fennel bulb lengthwise, removing the hard core. Place the fennel pieces on the grill and cook for 4–5 minutes on each side. When cooked, set aside in a bowl and keep warm.

2 Cook the pepper quarters on the skin side only for 5 minutes and add to the fennel slices.

3 Add the butter beans to the grilled vegetables. Crumble in the feta and add the toasted pine nuts, chopped parsley, olive oil, and a little salt and pepper. Toss, garnish with more parsley, and serve.

asparagus salad with tarragon and lemon dressing

3 tablespoons olive oil (optional)
1 lb asparagus
2/3 cup Tarragon and Lemon Dressing
   (see page 74)
2 cups arugula or other salad leaves
2 green onions, finely sliced
4 radishes, finely sliced
sea salt and black pepper

To garnish
roughly chopped herbs (such as
   tarragon, parsley, chervil, and dill)
thin strips of lemon zest

Serves 4
Preparation time 15 minutes
Cooking time about 5 minutes

This simple dish can be made in the morning and left to marinate all day, to serve at supper. Trim the ends of the asparagus stalks by cutting them across at a sharp angle just where the bright green color starts to fade into a dull green.

1 Heat the oil, if using, in a grill pan and add the asparagus in a single layer. Cook for about 5 minutes, turning occasionally. The asparagus should be tender when pierced with the tip of a sharp knife, and lightly patched with brown. Remove from the pan to a shallow dish and sprinkle with salt and pepper. Cover with the Tarragon and Lemon Dressing and toss gently, then let stand for 5 minutes.

2 Arrange the arugula on a platter, sprinkle the green onions and radishes over the top, and arrange the asparagus in a pile in the middle of the leaves. Garnish with chopped herbs and thin strips of lemon zest. Serve on its own with bread or as an accompaniment to a main dish.

eggplant, haloumi, and cumin bruschetta

1 tablespoon cumin seeds

1/4 cup extra virgin olive oil, plus extra
    for drizzling

grated zest of 1 lemon

2 small eggplants, each cut lengthwise
    into 4 slices

4 thick slices of day-old country bread

8 oz haloumi cheese, cut into 4 slices

2 garlic cloves, halved

2 cups arugula

Serves 4

Preparation time 10 minutes, plus
    infusing time

Cooking time 15–25 minutes

Haloumi is a sheep's milk cheese from Cyprus that grills particularly well, forming an attractive golden crust.

1 Toast the cumin seeds in a small skillet until they start to pop and give off a smoky aroma. Add the oil and lemon zest, remove from the heat, cover, and leave to infuse for a few hours.

2 Heat a grill pan over a medium heat. Cook the eggplant slices for 4–5 minutes on each side. Remove from the pan and dip each slice into the cumin-scented oil, reserving the remaining oil. Spread the eggplant slices on a plate and let cool to room temperature.

3 Just before serving, prepare the bruschetta. Heat the grill pan to a medium heat, add the bread, and toast each side well. Add the haloumi and cook on each side for 1–2 minutes, turning it carefully with a spatula.

4 Rub the toast all over with the cut garlic and drizzle with olive oil. Toss the arugula in the remaining cumin oil and heap on top of the bruschetta. Arrange slices of eggplant and haloumi over the arugula and serve immediately.

grilled thyme-marinated goat's milk cheeses

4 crottin de chevre, or small, firm goat's
   milk cheeses, halved horizontally
4 slices walnut bread

Marinade
1 scant cup extra virgin olive oil, plus
   extra if necessary
1/4 cup walnut oil
1 teaspoon dried thyme or lemon thyme
   sprigs
grated zest of 1 lemon
1 teaspoon crushed dried red chilies
1 small garlic clove, thinly sliced
8 black peppercorns
8 large grapevine leaves in brine,
   rinsed well in cold water

To serve
green salad
balsamic vinegar

Serves 4
Preparation time 10 minutes, plus
   marinating time
Cooking time about 7 minutes

1 Put all the marinade ingredients into a 1-pint screw-top jar and mix well. Add the halved goat's milk cheeses and let marinate in a cool place for at least 24 hours and up to 3 days.

2 Remove the cheeses from the marinade and drain on paper towels to remove any excess oil. Place the grape leaves on a cutting board and put half a goat's milk cheese in the center of each one. Wrap the leaves around the cheese so that it is sealed inside.

3 Heat a grill pan over a medium heat, then grill the walnut bread. Keep the bread warm. Place the 8 leaf parcels on the grill pan, seam side down, and cook for about 4–5 minutes, turning once, until the leaves are crispy and the cheese is melting.

4 Serve the goat's milk cheeses immediately with the grilled walnut bread and a little green salad, drizzled with the marinating oil and some balsamic vinegar.

open-faced vegetable tart with parmesan

1 red onion
1 red bell pepper
1 leek
2 flat mushrooms
1 small fennel bulb
1 small eggplant or 4 baby eggplants
1 zucchini
2 garlic cloves, peeled but left whole
1 bunch of basil
drizzle of olive oil
3/4 cup coarsely grated Parmesan
     cheese
sea salt and black pepper

Pastry
11/2 cups unbleached all-purpose flour
1/4 cup (1/2 stick) butter, softened and
     cut into small pieces
1 teaspoon dried mixed herbs, such as
     thyme, sage, rosemary, and/or
     marjoram
1/3 cup water
1/3 cup olive oil

Serves 4–6
Preparation time 20 minutes
Cooking time about 45 minutes

This tart is both delicious and easy, and various vegetables can be used, to your taste. Serve it hot or cold with a green salad.

1 Heat a grill pan over a medium heat. Grill the vegetables before making the pastry: cut them into wedges or halves and grill until lightly patched with black. Grill the garlic cloves whole, then slice them.

2 To make the pastry, put the flour in a food processor, add the butter, and process until the mixture resembles breadcrumbs. Add the herbs, water, and oil, and mix to form a dough. Knead the dough on a lightly floured work surface until smooth.

3 Preheat the oven to 400°F. Lightly grease a cookie sheet and gently press out the dough to form a circle about 10–12 inches in diameter.

4 Arrange the grilled vegetables over the dough, pressing them in gently. Strip the leaves from the basil, then press them into the dough. Drizzle with olive oil, season well with salt and pepper and sprinkle with Parmesan. Bake in the oven for 12–15 minutes, until the dough is risen and golden.

spicy zucchini fritters

1 lb zucchini, grated

1 egg, beaten

2 tablespoons unbleached all-purpose flour

1 jalapeño pepper, seeded and chopped

1 garlic clove, crushed

3 oz cheddar cheese, grated (about 1 cup)

sea salt and black pepper

dill sprigs, to garnish

Serves 4
Preparation time 10 minutes
Cooking time 20 minutes

These can be served as a side dish, or, for a really special treat, topped with smoked salmon and cream cheese and served as an appetizer.

1 Heat a grill pan over a medium heat. Squeeze the excess moisture out of the grated zucchini—the best way to do this is to put the zucchini into a clean tea towel and squeeze well.

2 In a bowl, mix together the egg and flour until smooth, add the jalapeño, garlic, cheddar, and zucchini, mix well, and season with salt and pepper to taste.

3 Spoon the mixture onto the grill, flatten it with a spatula, and cook the fritters for 4–5 minutes on one side. Do not disturb them while they are cooking, because a crust needs to form on the cooking side or they will be difficult to turn. Turn them over and cook for an additional 4–5 minutes on the second side.

4 Keep the cooked fritters warm and repeat until all the mixture has been used. Serve garnished with dill sprigs.

crispy parma ham parcels with blue cheese and pears

8 slices Parma ham or prosciutto
3 1/2 oz creamy blue cheese (such as
    Roquefort, Saint Agur, Dolcelatte, or
    Gorgonzola), cut into thin slices
1 teaspoon thyme leaves
1 pear, peeled and diced
1/4 cup shelled walnuts, chopped

To serve
watercress leaves tossed in olive oil
    and balsamic vinegar
1 pear, peeled, quartered, and sliced

Serves 4
Preparation time 10 minutes
Cooking time 4 minutes

1 Place a slice of Parma ham on a cutting board and then put a second slice across it to form a cross shape. Arrange one-quarter of the blue cheese slices in the center, scatter with some thyme, then top with some of the diced pear. Add a few walnuts, then fold over the sides of the ham to form a neat parcel. Repeat this process so that you have 4 parcels.

2 Heat a grill pan over a medium heat. Place the parcels on the grill and cook for about 2 minutes on each side until the ham is crisp and the cheese is beginning to ooze out of the sides.

3 Serve the parcels immediately with the dressed watercress leaves and slices of fresh pear.

chili-marinated butternut squash with frazzled chorizo

1 small butternut squash, peeled and
  cut into thin wedges
1 red onion, cut into quarters
1 red bell pepper, cored, seeded, and
  cut into thick strips
8 thin slices from a large salami-sized
  chorizo
lime juice, to serve

Chili marinade
 2–4 red chilies (depending on heat
  desired), seeded and finely
  chopped
2 garlic cloves, crushed
1 wide strip of lemon zest
1 bay leaf, torn
1/3 cup olive oil
2 tablespoons cider vinegar
2 tablespoons lime juice
sea salt and black pepper

Serves 4
Preparation time 10 minutes, plus
  marinating time
Cooking time 22 minutes

The chili marinade can be kept for at least two weeks in an airtight jar, so you can make more than you need and keep it for future use.

1 Thoroughly mix all the marinade ingredients and place in a large bowl with the butternut squash, onion, and red bell pepper. Toss to coat, then cover and set aside at room temperature for about an hour.

2 Heat a grill pan over a medium heat, then quickly grill the chorizo slices for 1 minute on each side, until crisp. Remove and drain on paper towels.

3 Shake off any excess marinade from the butternut squash wedges, then put them on the grill pan and cook for about 20 minutes, turning once. Add the pepper and onion for the last 3–4 minutes, so that they char lightly.

4 Serve immediately, sprinkled with the frazzled chorizo and a squeeze of lime juice.

fish and seafood

grilled miso cod with bok choy

4 chunky cod fillets, about 6 oz each
4 heads bok choy, halved lengthwise
    and blanched in boiling water for
    1–2 minutes
olive oil, for brushing

Miso sauce
1/2 cup miso paste
1/4 cup soy sauce
1/4 cup sake
1/4 cup rice wine (mirin)
1/4 cup sugar

Serves 4
Preparation time 10 minutes, plus
    marinating time
Cooking time 15–20 minutes

Miso is a fermented soybean paste from Japan, which can be used to marinate any type of firm white fish.

1 First make the miso sauce. Put the miso, soy sauce, sake, rice wine, and sugar into a small saucepan and heat gently until the sugar has dissolved. Simmer very gently for about 5 minutes, stirring frequently. Remove from the heat and set aside to cool.

2 Arrange the cod fillets in a snug-fitting dish and cover with the cold miso sauce. Rub the sauce over the fillets so that they are completely covered and let marinate for at least 6 hours, but preferably overnight.

3 Heat a grill pan over a medium heat and remove the cod fillets from the miso sauce. Place the fish on the grill and cook for about 2–3 minutes, then carefully turn them over and cook for an additional 2–3 minutes. Remove and keep warm.

4 Heat a clean grill pan and brush a little oil over the cut side of the bok choy. Place the bok choy, cut side down, on the grill and cook for about 2 minutes until hot and lightly charred. Arrange on a serving plate with the cod and serve immediately.

grilled bream with ginger and shallots

4 small bream, about 8 oz each,
    cleaned and scaled
steamed rice garnished with chopped
    cilantro, to serve

Marinade
1 bunch cilantro, chopped
2 shallots, finely chopped
1 2-inch piece fresh ginger, peeled and
    finely chopped
3 tablespoons mirin
2 tablespoons sesame oil
2 tablespoons light soy sauce
2 tablespoons lime juice
1 tablespoon fish sauce

Serves 4
Preparation time 10–15 minutes, plus
    infusing time
Cooking time 8–10 minutes

Other small fish such as snapper, sea bass, and monkfish can also be used for this recipe.

1 Put the bream on a cutting board and, using a sharp knife, make 3–4 diagonal slits in the flesh on both sides. Arrange the fish side by side in a shallow dish.

2 Mix together all the marinade ingredients and pour over the fish, using your hands to rub the marinade into the slits. Cover the dish and place in the refrigerator for 4 hours for the flavors to infuse.

3 Bring the fish back to room temperature for an hour, then heat a grill pan over a medium heat. Grill the fish for about 8–10 minutes, turning once, until they are cooked and the skins are crispy. Serve the bream immediately with steamed rice, garnished with chopped cilantro.

stuffed monkfish with balsamic dressing

1/2 cup balsamic vinegar

4 monkfish fillets, about 5 oz each

4 teaspoons good-quality tapenade

8 basil leaves

8 strips of bacon, stretched with the
 back of a knife

3/4 lb green beans

1 cup frozen peas

6 green onions, finely sliced

4 oz feta cheese, crumbled

2 tablespoons basil oil

sea salt

Serves 4
Preparation time 10–15 minutes
Cooking time 12–14 minutes

1 Pour the balsamic vinegar into a small saucepan. Bring to a boil over medium heat, then simmer for about 8–10 minutes until thick and glossy. Set aside to cool slightly, but keep warm.

2 Place the monkfish fillets on a cutting board and, using a sharp knife, make a deep incision about 2 inches long in the side of each fillet. Stuff with 1 teaspoon tapenade and 2 basil leaves. Wrap 2 strips of bacon around each fillet, sealing in the filling. Fasten with a toothpick.

3 Bring a pan of salted water to a boil, add the green beans, and cook for 3 minutes. Add the peas and cook for another minute. Drain and keep warm.

4 Heat a grill pan over a medium heat and place the monkfish directly on the grill. Cook for 4–5 minutes on each side until the fish are cooked. Set aside and let rest for a minute or two.

5 Meanwhile, toss the beans and peas with the green onions, feta, and basil oil, and arrange on serving plates. Top with a monkfish fillet and serve immediately, drizzled with the warm balsamic dressing.

salmon wrapped in parma ham with fontina cheese

4 4-oz salmon fillets, skinned

4 thin slices of fontina cheese

4 or 8 fresh bay leaves, depending
  on size

8 thin slices of Parma ham or
  prosciutto

sea salt and black pepper

fresh pasta or mixed salad, to serve

Serves 4
Preparation time 10 minutes
Cooking time 10 minutes

1 Heat a grill pan over a medium heat. Season the salmon fillets with salt and pepper to taste. Place each fillet on 2 slices of ham.

2 Trim any rind from the fontina and cut the cheese to fit on top of the fillets. Put the cheese on the salmon, then put the bay leaves on top of the cheese and wrap the ham around the salmon, securing the cheese and bay leaves. Fasten with a toothpick.

3 Cook the wrapped salmon fillets on the grill for 4–5 minutes on each side, taking care not to break them when turning them over. Serve with fresh pasta tossed in butter, or a leafy salad.

grilled salmon with a chili crust

3 teaspoons crushed dried red chilies
3 tablespoons sesame seeds
1 large bunch parsley, chopped
4 5-oz salmon fillets, skinned
1 egg white, lightly beaten
sea salt and black pepper

To serve
1 lime, cut into halves
noodles (optional)

Serves 4
Preparation time 10 minutes
Cooking time about 10 minutes

This chili crust not only looks good, but it also imparts some delicious flavors to the fish.

1 Heat a grill pan over a medium heat. Mix together the chilies, sesame seeds, parsley, salt and pepper, and sprinkle on a plate.

2 Dip the salmon fillets into the egg white, then coat them with the mixed crust ingredients. Pat the mixture onto the salmon to ensure an even coating.

3 Place the fillets on the hot grill and cook for 4 minutes on each side, turning them carefully with a spatula and keeping the crust on the fish. Grill the lime wedges for 2 minutes until charred. Serve the salmon with the grilled lime halves and with noodles, if you like.

grilled snapper with carrots and caraway seeds

1 lb carrots, sliced

2 teaspoons caraway seeds

4 6-oz snapper fillets

2 oranges

1 bunch cilantro, roughly chopped, plus
    extra to garnish

1/4 cup olive oil

sea salt and black pepper

Serves 4
Preparation time 10 minutes
Cooking time 15 minutes

1 Heat a grill pan over a medium heat and grill the carrots for 3 minutes on each side, adding the caraway seeds for the last 2 minutes of cooking. Transfer to a bowl and keep warm.

2 Cook the snapper fillets on the grill for 3 minutes on each side. Meanwhile, juice one of the oranges and cut the other into quarters. Place the orange quarters on the grill until browned.

3 Add the cilantro to the carrots and mix well. Season with salt and pepper to taste and stir in the olive oil and orange juice. Serve the cooked fish with the carrots and grilled orange wedges. Garnish with extra chopped cilantro.

trout with horseradish salad

4 6-oz trout fillets, skinned
2 oz fresh horseradish
1/2 cup red radishes
3 1/2 oz baby spinach leaves
5 tablespoons olive oil, plus extra
   for drizzling
2 tablespoons cider vinegar
sea salt and black pepper

Serves 4
Preparation time 10 minutes
Cooking time 8 minutes

Fresh horseradish keeps for several weeks in the crisper drawer of the refrigerator, but it starts to lose its pungency when it is grated. However, any leftover grated horseradish can be frozen.

1 Heat a grill pan over a medium heat. Place the trout fillets on the grill and cook for 4 minutes on each side. Do not attempt to turn the fillets over too soon or they will break.

2 Meanwhile, peel and grate the horseradish. Trim the radishes top and bottom and cut into quarters.

3 Toss the grated horseradish in a bowl with the radishes, spinach, olive oil, cider vinegar, and salt and pepper. Mix well and divide among 4 plates. Place the grilled trout on the salad, drizzle with a little olive oil, season with salt and pepper, and serve.

sardines stuffed with lemon

12 fresh sardines, gutted

2 lemons, cut into thin wedges

4 plum tomatoes, peeled and diced

1 red onion, sliced

3 tablespoons olive oil

sea salt and black pepper

2 tablespoons chopped flat-leaf
    parsley, to garnish

Serves 3 (or 4 as an appetizer)
Preparation time 10–14 minutes
Cooking time 10–12 minutes

1 Heat a grill pan over a medium heat. Rinse the sardines in cold water. Pat dry with paper towels. Stuff the stomach cavity of each sardine with a lemon wedge and secure with a toothpick.

2 Place the stuffed sardines on the grill and cook for 5–7 minutes on each side. Be careful when turning the sardines because they are fragile.

3 Arrange the tomatoes and red onion on a serving plate, drizzle with the olive oil, and sprinkle with salt and pepper.

4 When the sardines are cooked, remove the toothpicks and serve them on the tomato and onion salad. Garnish with parsley.

mediterranean swordfish skewers with peppers and mango

1 lb skinned swordfish steak, cut into large cubes

1 green bell pepper, cored, seeded, and cut into 1-inch pieces

1 red bell pepper, cored, seeded, and cut into 1-inch pieces

1 red onion, cut into quarters

1 ripe but firm mango, peeled and cut into thick slices

Marinade
2–3 thyme sprigs
leaves from 1–2 rosemary sprigs
grated zest of 1 lemon
1 garlic clove, lightly crushed
1/2 cup olive oil
2 teaspoons fennel seeds
black pepper

Fennel and olive salad
1 large fennel bulb, sliced very finely
3 1/2 oz good quality Kalamata olives, pitted
grated zest of 1 lemon
2 tablespoons olive oil
1 tablespoon lemon juice
sea salt and black pepper
fennel fronds, to garnish

Serves 4
Preparation time 20 minutes, plus marinating time
Cooking time about 5 minutes

Rather than using metal skewers, use bamboo skewers soaked in warm water for about 20 minutes, or sharpened rosemary sprigs with the leaves removed.

1 Mix together all the marinade ingredients and place in a large, shallow dish with the swordfish cubes, peppers, onion, and mango. Cover and set aside at room temperature for about 1 hour.

2 Arrange the fennel slices on a large serving plate and scatter with the olives and lemon zest.

3 Heat a grill pan over a medium heat. Thread the swordfish, peppers, onion, and mango onto the skewers. If you are using rosemary sprigs, cover any leaves that are still attached to the ends with a piece of foil to prevent them from burning. Place the skewers directly on the grill and cook for about 5 minutes, turning occasionally.

4 Drizzle olive oil and lemon juice over the fennel salad and scatter with the fennel fronds. Season well with salt and pepper and serve immediately with the swordfish skewers.

tuna with wasabi butter

1/2 cup (1 stick) butter, at room
 temperature
grated zest and juice of 1 lime
2 teaspoons wasabi paste
4 6-oz tuna steaks
sea salt and black pepper

Serves 4
Preparation time 5 minutes, plus
 chilling time
Cooking time 8 minutes

Wasabi is a Japanese herb. It is not related to horseradish but it has a similar flavor and pungency. Wasabi paste is available from Asian grocery stores.

1 Place the butter, lime zest and juice, and wasabi paste in a food processor and blend well. Spoon the butter onto wax paper, wrap the paper around it, and roll it into a sausage shape. Refrigerate for 30 minutes until firm.

2 Heat a grill pan over a medium heat and cook the tuna steaks for 4 minutes on each side. To get a crisscross effect, cook the steaks for 2 minutes over high heat, then give them a quarter turn and cook for another 2 minutes. Repeat for the other side. The steaks are done when firm to the touch and charred.

3 Cut the butter into 8 equal slices. Top each steak with 2 slices of butter and serve immediately.

arugula pesto mussels in parcels

2 lb mussels, scrubbed and debearded

Arugula pesto
1 cup arugula, roughly chopped
1 small garlic clove, finely chopped
1/3 cup olive oil
1 1/2 tablespoons pine nuts, lightly
   toasted
1 tablespoon freshly grated Parmesan
   cheese
1 tablespoon lemon juice
1/4 cup sour cream
sea salt and black pepper

Lemon breadcrumbs
1 small (1 1/2 oz) stale baguette, or other
   crusty bread
finely grated zest of 1/2 lemon
1 garlic clove, finely chopped
1 tablespoon olive oil
1 tablespoon chopped flat-leaf parsley
1/4 teaspoon crushed dried red chilies
   (optional)

To serve
cooked asparagus tips
crusty bread

Serves 2
Preparation time 20 minutes, plus
   preparing the mussels
Cooking time 15–20 minutes

1 To make the pesto, put the arugula, garlic, olive oil, and pine nuts into a food processor and blend until fairly smooth. Pour into a bowl and stir in the Parmesan, lemon juice, and sour cream. Season with salt and pepper to taste.

2 Put the stale bread into a clean, dry food processor and process into crumbs. Add the lemon zest, garlic, olive oil, parsley, and crushed chilies, if using, and mix well.

3 Heat a nonstick skillet over low heat and add the breadcrumb mixture. Toast gently for about 5 minutes, stirring frequently to prevent burning, until crisp and golden. Drain any excess oil by transferring the breadcrumbs to a plate lined with paper towels and let cool.

4 In a large bowl, mix the dry mussels with the pesto sauce until thoroughly coated, then divide between 2 large pieces of foil. Fold up the edges and scrunch them together to seal. Heat a grill pan over a medium heat, then put the foil parcels directly on the grill for about 15–20 minutes until the mussels have opened. Discard any that remain unopened.

5 Place the parcels, unopened, in warmed bowls. Diners open the parcels themselves and sprinkle the crispy breadcrumbs over the mussels. Serve with cooked asparagus tips and plenty of crusty bread.

lime, coconut, and chili-spiked squid

10–12 prepared baby squid, total weight about 12 oz including tentacles
4 limes, halved
mixed green salad, to serve

Dressing
2 red chilies, finely chopped
juice and grated zest of 2 limes
1 1-inch piece fresh ginger, peeled and grated
1/4 cup dried, creamed, or freshly grated coconut
1/4 cup peanut oil
1–2 tablespoons chili oil
1 tablespoon white wine vinegar

Serves 2
Preparation time 10 minutes, plus marinating time
Cooking time 4 minutes

If you don't have time to marinate the squid, just toss the pieces in the dressing before cooking and drizzle more over them before serving. Be careful not to overcook the squid, because they will quickly go rubbery and taste unpleasant.

1 Cut down the side of each squid so that they can be laid flat. Using a sharp knife, score the inside flesh lightly in a crisscross pattern.

2 Mix together all the dressing ingredients. Toss the squid in half the dressing and set aside for about an hour.

3 Heat a grill pan over a high heat, then place the limes, cut side down, on the pan and grill for about 2 minutes until nicely charred. Set aside.

4 Keeping the grill pan very hot, add the squid to the pan and cook quickly for 1 minute. Turn them over and cook for another minute until charred.

5 Place the squid on a cutting board and cut them into strips. Top with the remaining dressing and serve with the grilled limes and a mixed green salad.

sticky ginger shrimp

1 lb 10 oz large raw tiger shrimp,
    peeled and deveined
1 teaspoon vegetable oil
11/2-inch piece fresh ginger, peeled
    and finely chopped
2 garlic cloves, crushed
2 shallots, finely chopped
1/4 cup brown sugar
2 tablespoons water
2 tablespoons soy sauce
1 tablespoon distilled white vinegar
freshly cooked noodles, to serve

To garnish
shredded green onions
orange zest strips

Serves 4
Preparation time 10 minutes
Cooking time about 12–16 minutes

These shrimp taste delicious and make an impressive dish. Serve them with rice noodles or egg noodles.

1 Heat a grill pan over a medium heat. Put the shrimp on the grill and cook for 6–8 minutes, depending on their size. You may have to do this in batches.

2 Meanwhile, heat the oil in a small saucepan and add the ginger, garlic, and shallots. Cook for a few minutes but do not allow to brown. Add the brown sugar, water, soy sauce, and vinegar. Simmer gently for 3–5 minutes over low heat, and stir frequently so that the liquid evaporates to produce a rich coating sauce.

3 Serve the prawns on a nest of noodles with the sticky sauce drizzled over the top. Garnish with shredded green onions and orange zest.

seared scallops with slow-roasted tomatoes and crispy pancetta

8 small vine-ripened tomatoes, halved

2 garlic cloves, finely chopped

8 basil leaves

2 tablespoons olive oil

2 tablespoons balsamic vinegar

8 thin slices pancetta

16–20 king scallops, corals and muscles removed

8 good quality canned artichoke hearts in oil, halved

6 cups corn salad (lamb's lettuce), trimmed

sea salt and black pepper

Serves 4

Preparation time 10 minutes, plus cooling time

Cooking time about 1¹/₂ hours

1 Preheat the oven to 225°F. Arrange the tomatoes close together, cut side up, in a roasting pan. Scatter with the chopped garlic and basil, drizzle with 1 tablespoon each of the olive oil and balsamic vinegar, and season well with salt and pepper. Bake for 1¹/₂ hours.

2 Heat a grill pan over a high heat and grill the pancetta slices for about 2 minutes, turning once, until crisp and golden. Transfer to a plate lined with paper towels until needed.

3 Keeping the grill pan hot, quickly sear the scallops for 1 minute, then turn them over and cook for an additional minute on the other side until cooked and starting to caramelize. Remove from the grill, cover with foil, and let rest for 2 minutes while you grill the artichoke hearts until hot and charred.

4 Toss the corn salad with the remaining olive oil and balsamic vinegar and arrange on serving plates. Top with the artichokes, tomatoes, and cooked scallops. Crumble the crispy pancetta over the top and serve immediately.

garlicky lobster with lemon butter and mayonnaise

1 steamed lobster, about 2–3 lb
6 tablespoons (3/4 stick) butter, at room
  temperature
1 garlic clove, crushed
1 tablespoon capers in sea salt, rinsed
  and drained
1 tablespoon lemon juice
1 tablespoon chopped chervil
1 tablespoon chopped flat-leaf parsley
1 teaspoon chopped tarragon
buttery mashed potatoes, to serve

Mayonnaise
2 egg yolks, at room temperature
pinch of salt
1/2 cup peanut oil
1/2 cup mild olive oil
1 tablespoon lemon juice
1 teaspoon wholegrain mustard
salt and black pepper

Serves 2
Preparation time 20 minutes, plus time
  to prepare the lobster
Cooking time about 30 minutes

You can buy steamed lobsters from a fish market, but langoustine and jumbo shrimp also work very well if you prefer.

1 Using a very sharp knife, cut the lobster in half lengthwise and remove the intestinal vein that runs down the back. Crack the claws and set aside.

2 To make the mayonnaise, put the egg yolks in a bowl with a pinch of salt and whisk (an electric mixer fitted with a whisk attachment works best) for 1 minute until the eggs are frothy. Very slowly, add the peanut oil drop by drop until you have a thick glossy mixture. Now do the same with the olive oil, whisking continuously until all the oil has been incorporated. Still whisking, drizzle in the lemon juice and the mustard. Season with salt and pepper to taste.

3 Heat a grill pan over a high heat. Mix 2 tablespoons of the butter with the garlic and rub the lobster flesh with the garlicky butter. Lay the shell side of the lobster on the grill for 3–4 minutes, then turn it onto the cut side and cook for 2 minutes until the flesh and claws are hot and charred. Remove from the grill and keep warm while you prepare the lemon butter.

4 Melt the remaining butter in a small skillet and heat until it begins to turn golden and smells nutty. Stir in the capers, lemon juice, and herbs, then remove from the heat.

5 Serve the lobster halves with the lemon caper butter and a small dish of the homemade mayonnaise.

meat and poultry

hot and sour beef noodles

1 tablespoon Szechuan peppercorns,
    lightly crushed
13 oz sirloin steak, about 2 inches thick
7 oz rice vermicelli noodles, soaked in
    boiling water
1 red bell pepper, cored, seeded, and
    cut into thin strips
6 green onions, finely sliced
2 cups bean sprouts

Dressing
1/4 cup lime juice
1/4 cup rice wine vinegar
2 lemongrass stalks, outer leaves
    removed and finely sliced
2 red chilies, seeded and finely sliced
2 tablespoons Thai fish sauce
2 tablespoons dark brown sugar
2 tablespoons light soy sauce

To garnish
1 cucumber, cut into very fine strips
    lengthwise, ideally on a mandolin
1 small bunch mint, separated into
    leaves
1 tablespoon lightly toasted sesame
    seeds

Serves 4
Preparation time 20 minutes
Cooking time about 2 minutes

A thick-cut tenderloin steak or a top loin (strip) steak could also be used for this recipe. Allow the same cooking times.

1 Heat a grill pan over a high heat. Sprinkle the peppercorns on a plate, then press the steak firmly into the peppercorns until it is covered. Place the steak on the grill pan and cook for about 1 minute on each side, or longer if you prefer. Transfer to a cutting board and allow to rest for a few minutes, then cut into very thin slices.

2 Mix together all the ingredients for the dressing. Mix 2 tablespoons with the cucumber strips.

3 In a large bowl, toss the sliced steak with the noodles, red bell pepper, green onions, bean sprouts, mint leaves, sesame seeds, and the remaining dressing.

4 Divide the mixture among 4 warmed plates and scatter with the dressed cucumber strips.

teriyaki steak

1½ lb thick-cut sirloin steak
stir-fried noodles and vegetables,
   to serve

Teriyaki marinade
scant 1/2 cup pineapple juice
1/4 cup soy sauce
2 garlic cloves, crushed
11/4-inch piece fresh ginger, peeled
   and finely chopped

Serves 4
Preparation time 5 minutes, plus
   marinating time
Cooking time 6–16 minutes

Thought to have Polynesian origins, teriyaki is a popular Japanese marinade. The complex flavors of soy sauce and ginger penetrate the meat with very tasty results.

1 Mix together all the ingredients for the marinade. Place the sirloin steak in a shallow dish and cover with the marinade. Turn the steak to coat it well. Cover and refrigerate for 24 hours, turning the meat as frequently as possible.

2 Heat a grill pan over a high heat. Cook the steak for 3 minutes on each side for rare, 5 minutes for medium, or 8 minutes for well done. Remove when cooked to your liking.

3 Allow to rest for a few minutes, then slice thinly. Serve on a bed of stir-fried noodles and vegetables.

red-hot hamburgers

1 lb 3 oz ground beef
2 garlic cloves, crushed
1 red onion, finely chopped
1 red chili, finely chopped
1 bunch parsley, chopped
1 tablespoon Worcestershire sauce
1 egg, beaten
4 Kaiser rolls or wholegrain hamburger
    buns, split
spicy greens, such as arugula
    or mizuna
1 beefsteak tomato, sliced
sea salt and black pepper
relish, to serve

Serves 4
Preparation time 10 minutes
Cooking time 6–14 minutes

These burgers can also be made with ground lamb and served in pita bread, if preferred.

1 Put the ground beef into a large bowl. Add the garlic, red onion, red chili, parsley, Worcestershire sauce, beaten egg, and a little salt and pepper. Mix well.

2 Heat a grill pan over a high heat. Divide the ground beef mixture into 4 pieces and shape into burgers. Place the burgers on the grill and cook for 3 minutes on each side for rare, 5 minutes for medium, or 7 minutes for well done.

3 Grill the bun halves quickly on a clean hot grill pan. Fill each bun with some greens, sliced tomato, and a grilled burger. Serve with some relish.

t-bone steak with caper butter and baby potatoes

2 T-bone steaks, about 10 oz each
12 oz cooked baby new potatoes
1 tablespoon olive oil
sea salt and black pepper

Caper butter
6 tablespoons (3/4 stick) butter
2 anchovy fillets in oil, drained
1 tablespoon capers, washed and
    drained
1 tablespoon lemon juice
1 tablespoon chopped flat-leaf parsley
1 tablespoon chopped chives
black pepper

Serves 2
Preparation time 10 minutes
Cooking time about 12 minutes

1 First make the caper butter. Put all the ingredients into a food processor and blend until fairly smooth. Scrape into a bowl with a spatula.

2 Heat a grill pan over a high heat, season the steaks with salt and pepper and place directly on the grill for about 3 minutes on each side, or to your liking. Cover and let rest in a warm place for about 5 minutes.

3 Meanwhile, toss the baby potatoes in the olive oil, season with salt and pepper, and place onto the grill pan. Cook over medium heat for 3–4 minutes, using tongs to turn them, until golden and heated through.

4 Put the steaks on warmed plates, place a little caper butter on top of each one, and serve immediately with the potatoes.

grilled italian lamb with rosemary oil

lamb loin roast, about 1¹/2 lb, trimmed
   of fat
4 garlic cloves, cut into slivers
a few small sprigs of rosemary
2 red onions, quartered
¹/4 cup olive oil
1 tablespoon chopped rosemary
sea salt and black pepper

To serve
fresh pasta
Parmesan cheese shavings

Serves 4
Preparation time 10 minutes
Cooking time 20–40 minutes

*Loin roasts are lean and tender, and easily absorb the delicious flavors of garlic
and rosemary.*

1 Heat a grill pan over a high heat. Make small incisions all over the loin roast
and insert the garlic slivers and rosemary sprigs. Place on the grill pan and cook,
turning occasionally, until charred all over, for about 10 minutes for rare,
or about 20 minutes for well done. Add the onions for the last 10 minutes and
char on the outside. Let the lamb rest for 5 minutes, then carve into slices.

2 Meanwhile, place the oil and the chopped rosemary in a mortar and crush with
a pestle to release the flavors. Season with salt and pepper. Spoon the rosemary
oil over the lamb slices and serve at once with the grilled onions. Serve with
fresh pasta, lightly tossed in olive oil, and Parmesan shavings.

sweet sticky spare ribs

1 side pork spare ribs, about 1 1/2 lb

Marinade
1 small onion, finely chopped
1 garlic clove, crushed
1-inch piece fresh ginger, peeled and
   freshly grated
1/3 cup cider vinegar
1/3 cup cola flavoured drink
2 tablespoons ketchup
1 tablespoon Worcestershire sauce
1 tablespoon dark soft brown sugar
1 tablespoon maple syrup
1/2 teaspoon Tabasco sauce
1/2 teaspoon smoked sweet paprika
1/2 teaspoon oregano
1/2 teaspoon ground cumin
1/2 teaspoon ground coriander
sea salt and black pepper

To serve
baked potatoes
homemade coleslaw

Serves 2
Preparation time 15 minutes, plus
   cooling and marinating time
Cooking time about 30 minutes

1 Place all the marinade ingredients in a small saucepan and heat slowly until just boiling. Reduce the heat and simmer gently for 8–10 minutes, then set aside to cool.

2 Cut the side of pork ribs into 4 pieces and arrange in a large, shallow dish. Cover with the cold marinade, making sure the pork is well coated. Cover and refrigerate for 12 hours or overnight.

3 Heat a grill pan over a medium heat and place the ribs on the grill. Cook the ribs for about 20 minutes, turning occasionally, until cooked through and sticky. While they are cooking, place the remaining marinade in a small pan on the stove and simmer gently for 10–15 minutes until thick and glossy.

4 Separate the ribs and serve with baked potatoes, homemade coleslaw, and the hot marinade.

turkish sausages with cracked wheat salad

Cracked wheat salad

1/2 cup coarse bulghur wheat, soaked
   in hot water for 20 minutes
4 green onions, finely chopped
1 green bell pepper, diced
1 tomato, seeded and diced
1 small bunch parsley, finely chopped
1 small bunch mint, finely chopped
1/4 cucumber, halved, seeded, and
   finely diced
3 tablespoons olive oil
2 tablespoons lemon juice
1 teaspoon sumac
sea salt and black pepper

Sausages

1 green bell pepper, cored, seeded,
   and roughly chopped
1 large green chili, roughly chopped
1/2 red onion, chopped
1 garlic clove, chopped
1 small bunch mint, chopped
1 small bunch parsley, chopped
2 tablespoons lemon juice
2 teaspoons sumac
1 teaspoon crushed red pepper
1 lb ground pork
salt and black pepper
large green chilies and Turkish bread,
   to serve

Serves 4
Preparation time 25 minutes,
   plus standing
Cooking time 13–16 minutes

Sumac is a rusty red, acidic-tasting spice, popular in Middle Eastern cooking. If you cannot find it, use the same amount of lemon juice.

1 Drain the bulghur wheat and put it in a large bowl with all the remaining salad ingredients and stir well. Set aside for 20 minutes to allow the flavors to develop.

2 Put all the sausage ingredients except the pork in a food processor and blend until very finely chopped but not pureed. Pour into a bowl, add the pork and some salt and pepper, and mix well with your hands.

3 Shape the mixture into 4 thick sausages, about 6 inches long, place on a cutting board, and flatten slightly.

4 Heat a grill pan over a high heat and grill the chilies for 5–6 minutes until softened and charred. Keep warm until needed. Place the pork sausages on the grill and cook for 8–10 minutes, turning once, until cooked through.

5 Serve the sausages immediately on a bed of cracked wheat salad with soft Turkish-style bread and the grilled green chilies.

pepper-crusted loin of venison

loin of venison weighing 1 1/2 lb, cut
   from the haunch
1/3 cup mixed peppercorns, crushed
2 tablespoons juniper berries, crushed
1 egg white, lightly beaten
sea salt and black pepper

To serve
redcurrant jelly
sweet potato chips
green beans

Serves 4
Preparation time 10 minutes
Cooking time up to 45 minutes

1 Make sure that the venison fits into your grill pan: if necessary, cut the loin in
half to fit. Heat a grill pan over a high heat.

2 Mix together the peppercorns, juniper berries, and salt, and place in a large
shallow dish. Dip the venison into the egg white, then roll it in the peppercorn
mixture, covering it evenly all over.

3 Cook the venison on the grill for 4 minutes on each side, turning it carefully so
that the crust stays intact. Cook evenly on all sides, then transfer the loin to a
lightly greased roasting pan and cook in a preheated oven, 400°F, for another
15 minutes for rare, and up to 30 minutes for well done. The exact time depends
on the thickness of the loin of venison.

4 Let the venison rest for a few minutes, then slice thickly and serve with green
beans, redcurrant jelly, and finely sliced sweet potato chips.

quail with sugar snap peas and baby corn

2 quails, partly boned, or spatchcocked
   (see right)
1/2 cup sugar snap peas
1/2 cup baby corn, halved lengthwise
1 garlic clove, smashed
1 tablespoon vegetable oil
2 teaspoons sesame oil
2 teaspoons light soy sauce

Marinade
1 small shallot, chopped
1 1-inch piece fresh ginger, peeled and
   grated
1 tablespoon pomegranate syrup
1 tablespoon sweet soy sauce
1 tablespoon brown rice vinegar
1/2 tablespoon tamarind paste
1 teaspoon Chinese five-spice powder

Serves 2
Preparation time 10 minutes, plus
   marinating time
Cooking time about 12 minutes

It is probably simplest to ask your butcher to spatchcock the quails for you, but if you wish to do it yourself, follow these instructions: remove the backbone, snip off the wing tips, and flatten the bird with the palm of your hand.

1 Mix together all the marinade ingredients in a large bowl. Add the quails and cover thoroughly with the marinade. Cover and place in the refrigerator for at least 8 hours, but preferably 24 hours.

2 Heat a grill pan over a medium heat. Place the quails directly on the grill and cook for about 8–10 minutes, turning once and basting regularly with the marinade. Once the quails are cooked through and sticky, remove them from the grill, cover with foil, and keep warm.

3 Place a clean, dry grill pan over high heat. Toss the sugar snap peas and baby corn in a bowl with the garlic and vegetable oil and then pour them onto the grill pan. Cook quickly for 2 minutes, moving them occasionally so they don't stick. Pour them back into the bowl, toss with the sesame oil and soy sauce, and serve immediately, topped with the sticky grilled quail and any juices.

grilled duck with oranges and cranberries

4 duck breasts
buttery mashed potatoes, to serve

Sauce
2 oranges
1/2 cup cranberries
1/4 cup light brown sugar
1 tablespoon honey
sea salt and black pepper

Serves 4
Preparation time 10 minutes
Cooking time 15 minutes

1 Heat a grill pan over a medium heat. Score the skin of the duck breasts through to the flesh—this allows the fat to be released and the skin to get crispy.

2 Place the duck breasts on the grill pan, skin side down, and cook for 6–10 minutes, then turn them over and cook on the other side for 4–6 minutes.

3 Meanwhile, remove the peel and pith from the oranges and cut them into segments. Place the oranges, cranberries, and sugar in a saucepan with salt and pepper to taste and simmer until the cranberries are soft. Stir in the honey.

4 Remove the duck from the grill, cut it into slices, and pour over the orange and cranberry sauce. Serve with mashed potatoes, if liked.

cajun blackened chicken with avocado salad

4 boneless chicken breasts, skin on,
about 5 oz each
Lebanese-style flatbread, pita bread, or
flour tortillas, to serve

Cajun seasoning
2 teaspoons paprika
2 teaspoons cayenne pepper
2 teaspoons dried oregano
2 teaspoons dried thyme
1 teaspoon garlic powder or granules
1 teaspoon onion powder or flakes
1 teaspoon cumin powder
1 teaspoon salt
1/2 teaspoon crushed black pepper

Avocado salad
1 small ripe but firm avocado, peeled,
pitted, and diced
1 small red onion, halved and finely
sliced
1 small red bell pepper, cored, seeded,
and finely sliced
1 large beefsteak tomato, quartered,
seeded, and sliced
2 tablespoons roughly chopped
flat-leaf parsley
2 tablespoons lemon juice
2 tablespoons olive oil
sea salt and black pepper

Serves 4
Preparation time 20 minutes, plus
marinating time
Cooking time 12 minutes

The chicken will get quite smoky as it cooks, but don't panic—this adds to the characteristic smoky flavors of Cajun cooking. This dish also works extremely well on the outdoor grill.

1 Score the skin of each chicken breast 3–4 times with a sharp knife. Mix together all the Cajun seasoning ingredients, then rub the mixture generously over the chicken breasts. Cover and set aside for at least 1 hour.

2 Heat a grill pan over a high heat. Place the chicken breasts on the grill, skin-side down, and cook for 4–5 minutes until the skins are blackened and crisp, then flip them over and cook for 3–4 minutes until cooked through. Remove the chicken breasts from the pan, cover with foil, and set aside to rest for 2–3 minutes.

3 Place the flatbread on the grill for 2–3 minutes, turning once, until warm and charred. Arrange on serving plates.

4 Mix together all the ingredients for the avocado salad and pile on top of the flatbreads. Cut the chicken into thick slices, reserving any juices.

5 Arrange the sliced chicken on top of the salad and serve immediately, drizzled with any remaining juices.

chicken and bacon caesar salad
with garlic croutons

4 boneless, skinless chicken breasts,
    about 5 oz each
1/4 cup olive oil, plus extra for chicken
1 ciabatta loaf, split lengthwise
2 garlic cloves, cut in half
8 strips bacon
4–6 small Romaine lettuce hearts,
    thickly sliced
salt and black pepper
Parmesan cheese shavings, to serve

Dressing
2 egg yolks
3 tablespoons lemon juice
1/4 teaspoon Worcestershire sauce
scant 1 cup olive oil
10 anchovy fillets in oil
1/4 cup freshly grated Parmesan
    cheese
black pepper

Serves 4
Preparation time 20 minutes
Cooking time 10–12 minutes

1   Place the chicken breasts between two pieces of plastic wrap and flatten with a rolling pin. Rub with olive oil and salt and pepper, and set aside.

2   To make the dressing, whisk together the egg yolks and lemon juice in a bowl, then add the Worcestershire sauce. Slowly drizzle in the olive oil, whisking continuously until all the oil has been added. Mash the anchovy fillets into the dressing with the back of a fork, then stir in the Parmesan and season with black pepper. Cover and chill until needed.

3   Heat a grill pan over a medium heat. Brush the ciabatta bread with the olive oil and place on the grill pan for about 2 minutes on each side until toasted and charred. Remove from the pan and immediately rub both sides with the cut garlic cloves. Cut the bread into thick strips and keep them warm.

4   Place the chicken on the grill for 3–4 minutes, turning once, until cooked through. Let rest while you grill the bacon for 2–3 minutes until crisp, turning once. Drain on paper towels, cut into large pieces and set aside.

5   In a large bowl, combine the Romaine lettuce with 4–6 tablespoons of the dressing, toss well to coat the leaves and divide among 4 bowls. Cut the chicken into slices and add to the salad with the bacon pieces and garlic croutons. Serve immediately with Parmesan shavings and the remaining dressing.

thai chicken breasts with fiery dipping sauce

4 boneless, skinless chicken breasts,
   about 5 oz each, cut into thin strips
8 bamboo skewers
steamed rice, to serve
cilantro sprigs, to garnish

Marinade
4 Kaffir lime leaves, shredded
2 lemongrass stalks, trimmed of outer
   leaves and thinly sliced
2 garlic cloves, roughly chopped
1 1-inch piece fresh ginger, peeled
   and finely grated
1 fresh red chili, finely sliced
1/2 cup peanut oil
3 tablespoons chopped cilantro leaves
2 tablespoons lime juice
1 tablespoon Thai fish sauce
1 tablespoon light soy sauce

Dipping sauce
1 red chili, seeded and finely chopped
1 Kaffir lime leaf, shredded
scant 1 cup coconut milk
2 tablespoons smooth peanut butter
1 tablespoon freshly grated ginger
1 tablespoon Thai red curry paste
1/2 tablespoon Thai fish sauce
1/2 tablespoon light soy sauce

Serves 4
Preparation time 25 minutes,
   plus marinating time
Cooking time 11–13 minutes

1 Mix together all the marinade ingredients in a bowl and add the chicken strips. Cover and chill in the refrigerator for at least 2 hours.

2 Meanwhile, make the dipping sauce. Combine all the ingredients in a small saucepan and simmer gently for about 5 minutes. Keep warm. Soak 8 bamboo skewers in warm water for at least 10 minutes.

3 Heat a grill pan over a medium heat. Remove the chicken from the marinade and thread them onto the bamboo skewers in an S-shape. Place on the grill pan for 6–8 minutes, turning once, until cooked through.

4 Serve the chicken skewers with steamed rice and the dipping sauce in a bowl or drizzled over the chicken. Garnish with cilantro sprigs and serve immediately.

mozzarella, sun-dried tomato, and sage-stuffed chicken

4 boneless, skinless chicken breasts,
   about 5 oz each
5 oz buffalo mozzarella, cut into
   8 slices
8 sun-dried tomatoes in oil, drained
   and sliced
6 sage leaves, finely sliced
finely grated zest of 1/2 lemon
olive oil, for rubbing
sea salt and black pepper

To serve
Fresh Tomato Sauce (see page 74)
steamed broccoli florets
crusty bread

Serves 4
Preparation time 15 minutes, plus
   freezing time
Cooking time 8–10 minutes

1 Place the chicken breasts in the freezer for 15 minutes, as this will make them easier to cut. Heat a grill pan over a medium heat.

2 Place the chicken breasts on a cutting board and, holding a sharp knife parallel to the work surface and beginning on a long side, cut them almost in half horizontally (not all the way through), so that you can open them as though you were opening a book. Arrange the mozzarella slices on one side of each breast, add the sun-dried tomatoes, sage, and lemon zest, and season well with salt and pepper. Fold the other side of the chicken breast over the cheese, so that the filling is sandwiched in. Rub with a little olive oil and set aside.

3 Place the chicken breasts on the grill pan and cook for 4–5 minutes on each side, until the cheese has melted and the chicken is cooked and golden. Let the chicken breasts rest for 1 minute, then cut them in half diagonally.

4 Serve the chicken on a bed of tomato sauce, with the freshly steamed broccoli florets and lots of crusty bread.

grilled turkey with exotic fruits

4 6-oz turkey breast cutlets
2 mangoes
wild and long grain rice, tossed with
   herbs, to serve

Passion fruit dressing
3 passion fruit
3 tablespoons olive oil
1 tablespoon white wine vinegar
sea salt and black pepper

Serves 4
Preparation time 15 minutes
Cooking time 40 minutes

This is an excellent dish for a summer garden party. Instead of stacking the grilled turkey and mango slices as directed here, simply chop them into chunks when cooked, toss them in a bowl with the passion fruit dressing, and serve. Passion fruit are available at Latino markets and some supermarkets.

1   Place the turkey cutlets between 2 pieces of plastic wrap and flatten with a rolling pin. Try to get them as thin as possible—about 1/4-inch thick is ideal. Cut each cutlet into 3 even-sized pieces.

2   Heat a grill pan over a medium heat. Peel the skin from the mangoes and cut 3 slices from either side of the stone. Place the mango slices on the grill and cook for 4 minutes on each side or until grill marks appear on the mango. Remove and keep warm in a low oven.

3   Place the flattened turkey pieces on the grill and cook in batches for 5 minutes on each side. Keep the grilled pieces warm while you cook the remainder.

4   Cut the passion fruit in half, scoop out the seeds, and place in a bowl. Add the olive oil, vinegar, and salt and pepper, and mix well.

5   To serve, stack the slices of turkey and mango in alternate layers on 4 individual plates and pour the passion fruit dressing over the top. Serve with a mixture of wild and long grain rice with herbs tossed through.

sauces, butters, and marinades

lemon pesto

1/3 cup pine nuts, toasted
1 large bunch basil
2 garlic cloves, crushed
1/3 cup freshly grated Parmesan
  cheese
grated zest and juice of 2 lemons
1/4 cup olive oil
sea salt and black pepper

Serves 4
Preparation time 10 minutes, plus
  cooling time
Cooking time 2–3 minutes

The addition of the grated zest and juice of two lemons adds an interesting piquancy to the classic basil pesto.

1 To toast the pine nuts, place them on a hot grill pan for 2–3 minutes, shaking it and moving the pine nuts around with a wooden spoon, so that they brown evenly. Allow to cool.

2 Process the pine nuts, basil, garlic, Parmesan, lemon zest and juice, olive oil, and salt and pepper in a food processor until smooth.

red wine marinade

1 onion, thinly sliced
1 carrot, thinly sliced
1 celery stalk, finely chopped
1 garlic clove, minced
1/2 cup red wine
2 tablespoons lemon juice
6 black peppercorns, bruised
1 bay leaf
sprig of parsley
sprig of thyme

Makes about 1 cup
Preparation time 10 minutes

This marinade imparts a rich and fruity flavor to meat and is particularly good with beef, lamb, and game.

Combine all the ingredients in a bowl and stir thoroughly. Add the food to be marinated and leave for the time given in the recipe. Use any excess marinade to baste the food during cooking.

fresh tomato sauce

2 tablespoons olive oil
1 garlic clove, finely chopped
1 13-oz can chopped Italian tomatoes
finely grated zest of 1/2 lemon
1/2 teaspoon dried oregano
1/4 teaspoon sugar
sea salt and black pepper

Serves 4
Preparation time 5 minutes
Cooking time 25–30 minutes

Heat the olive oil in a small saucepan and gently fry the garlic for 30 seconds. Add the chopped tomatoes, lemon zest, oregano, and sugar, and season with salt and pepper. Bring to a boil and simmer very gently for about 25 minutes, until the sauce is rich and thick.

tarragon and lemon dressing

finely grated zest of 1 lemon
2 tablespoons tarragon vinegar
1 tablespoon chopped tarragon
1/4 teaspoon Dijon mustard
pinch of sugar
5 tablespoons olive oil
salt and black pepper

Makes about 1/4 cup
Preparation time 5 minutes

Combine the lemon zest, vinegar, tarragon, mustard, and sugar in a small bowl and add salt and pepper to taste. Stir to mix, then gradually whisk in the oil. Alternatively, mix all the ingredients in a jar with a screw-top lid and shake well to combine.

ginger and herb butter

6 tablespoons (3/4 stick) butter
11/2 tablespoons chopped chervil
1 tablespoon orange juice
11/2 teaspoons grated fresh ginger
1 teaspoon grated orange zest
1 teaspoon honey
sea salt and black pepper

Serves 4–6
Preparation time 5 minutes, plus
   softening and chilling time

Remove the butter from the refrigerator about 30 minutes before you want to make the herb butter.

1 Process the butter in a food processor or blender to soften, or pound it using a mortar and pestle until it is creamy. Then add all the other ingredients and mix well. Place the mixture on a square of wax paper, form into a log shape, wrap tightly, and chill in the refrigerator until firm.

2 Serve with grilled fish fillets, such as salmon or monkfish. It is also good with grilled baby carrots.

thyme butter

6 tablespoons (3/4 stick) butter
3 tablespoons chopped thyme
3 teaspoons grated lemon zest
1/2 teaspoon cayenne pepper
1/2 teaspoon sea salt

Serves 4
Preparation time 5 minutes, plus
   infusing time
Cooking time 2–3 minutes

Use this flavored butter on lamb chops or sea bass fillets, or vegetables such as zucchini.

Melt the butter in a small saucepan and cook the thyme, lemon zest, cayenne pepper, and salt over a gentle heat for 2–3 minutes until softened. Let infuse for about 30 minutes before serving over grilled food.

harissa

4 red bell peppers
4 large red chilies
2 garlic cloves, crushed
5 tablespoons olive oil, plus extra
    to preserve
1 teaspoon caraway seeds
1/2 teaspoon cilantro leaves

Makes 1 small jar
Preparation time 10 minutes
Cooking time 25 minutes

This spicy Moroccan condiment is ideal with North African meat and fish dishes.
You can also add it to soups or spread it on bread.

1 Heat a grill pan over a high heat. Add the whole red bell peppers and cook for
15 minutes, turning occasionally. The skin will blacken and start to bubble.
Transfer the peppers to a plastic bag and set aside for 5 minutes. (This process
encourages the peppers to sweat, which makes it easier to remove their skins.)
When cool enough to handle, remove the skins, cores, and seeds from the
peppers and place the flesh in a food processor.

2 Grill the chilies for 10 minutes and remove the skin, cores, and seeds in the
same way. Add the chili flesh to the food processor with the garlic, olive oil,
caraway seeds, and cilantro. Process to a smooth paste.

3 If not used immediately, place the harissa in a container and pour a thin layer of
olive oil over the top. Cover with a lid and refrigerate until needed.

orange marinade

juice and finely grated zest of 1 orange
1 1/2-inch piece fresh ginger, peeled
    and finely chopped
3 tablespoons honey
1 tablespoon dark soy sauce
sea salt and black pepper

Makes about 1/4 cup
Preparation time 5 minutes

This is a good marinade for Asian dishes, particularly those using chicken and
fish. To make a lemon or lime marinade, substitute their juice and grated zest for
the orange.

Mix together all the ingredients in a bowl. Place chicken pieces or fish in a
shallow dish and rub in the marinade. Allow to marinate for at least 6 hours, but
preferably overnight.

desserts

grilled biscotti with lime sorbet and frozen vodka

2 eggs

1/2 cup superfine sugar

13/4 cups all-purpose flour

1/2 cup plus 2 tablespoons ground almonds or hazelnuts

1 heaping teaspoon baking powder

grated zest of 2 limes

pinch of salt

1/4 cup shelled pistachio nuts, roughly chopped

1/4 cup chopped hazelnuts

To serve

good-quality lime sorbet

vodka, placed in the freezer overnight

Makes about 30 biscotti

Preparation time 20 minutes

Cooking time 43–48 minutes, plus cooling time

1 Preheat the oven to 350°F. Whisk the eggs and sugar in a bowl until pale and frothy. Using a wooden spoon, slowly work in the flour, ground almonds, baking powder, grated lime zest, and salt. Add the chopped pistachio nuts and knead gently until you have a soft dough. Form the dough into a thick sausage shape, about 10 inches long and 4 inches wide, then flatten it slightly with the palm of your hand.

2 Transfer the dough to a greased cookie sheet and bake for 35–40 minutes until light golden. Remove from the oven and let cool for 5 minutes, then cut into 1/4-inch thick slices with a serrated knife.

3 Heat a grill pan over very low heat. Arrange the biscotti directly on the grill pan and cook for about 4 minutes on each side until crisp and golden. Transfer to a wire rack to cool.

4 To make a dramatic dessert, serve 2 scoops of lime sorbet in an attractive bowl or glass and top with a shot of frozen vodka. Arrange 2 biscotti on the edge of the bowl and serve immediately.

sweet bruschetta with plums and cinnamon

8 plums, more if they are small
4 slices white bread
2/3 cup plain yogurt
ground cinnamon, to dust

Caramel sauce
6 tablespoons (3/4 stick) butter
scant 1/2 cup brown sugar
3 tablespoons water

Serves 4
Preparation time 10 minutes
Cooking time 10–15 minutes

This makes a delicious dessert, especially during the summer months when plums are at their best.

1 Put the butter, sugar, and water in a small saucepan and simmer for 5 minutes to make a smooth caramel sauce. Remove from the heat and set aside.

2 Heat a grill pan over a medium heat. If the plums are large, cut them in half and remove the pits; if they are small leave them whole. Place the plums on the grill and cook for 5 minutes, turning constantly.

3 Toast the slices of bread on the grill pan. Arrange the toast on 4 plates and add the grilled plums and plain yogurt. Top with the caramel sauce and dust the plums with cinnamon.

grilled panettone with peaches and cream

4 peaches, halved and pitted
4 slices panettone (sweet Italian egg
   bread with fruit)
ground cinnamon
1/4 cup whipped cream
confectioner's sugar, to garnish

Serves 4
Preparation time 5 minutes
Cooking time 10–15 minutes

Other fruits, such as apples, apricots, and pears, can be grilled and used instead of the peaches, if you like.

1 Heat a grill pan over a medium heat and cook the peaches for about 5 minutes on each side until lightly charred.

2 Place the panettone on the grill pan and toast for 1–2 minutes on each side, until golden brown.

3 Place the peaches on the panettone and dust with cinnamon. Spoon on the whipped cream, sprinkle with confectioner's sugar, and serve immediately.

buttered croissants with sweetened chestnut cream

6 tablespoons (3/4 stick) unsalted butter

4 1-day-old croissants, split in half
  horizontally

4 teaspoons raw sugar

1/2 cup sweetened chestnut puree

1/2 cup mascarpone cheese (Italian
  cream cheese available at many
  supermarkets)

2 tablespoons plain yogurt

1 tablespoon honey, plus extra
  for drizzling

To garnish
chopped marrons glaces (optional)
crushed chocolate-covered coffee
  beans, to garnish (optional)

Serves 4
Preparation time 10 minutes
Cooking time 5 minutes

This doesn't have to be served as a dessert, so why not try it as a mid-afternoon treat or a late-night snack? For a summer variation, omit the chestnut puree and serve with fresh mixed berries.

1 Melt the butter gently in a small saucepan. Brush it over the cut sides of the croissants, then sprinkle them with the raw sugar. Set aside.

2 In a bowl, beat the chestnut puree with the mascarpone cheese, yogurt, and honey until smooth.

3 Heat a grill pan over a low heat. Place the croissants, cut side down, on the grill and toast gently for 2–3 minutes until hot and golden.

4 Transfer to serving plates, top with some chestnut cream, and drizzle with a little extra honey. Sprinkle with a few chopped marrons glaces or crushed chocolate coffee beans, if you like, and serve immediately.

chocolate, date, and almond panini

1/4 cup whole blanched almonds
3 oz good-quality white chocolate,
   finely grated
8 soft dates, pitted and chopped
1/4 cup sliced almonds, lightly toasted
8 slices brioche, buttered on both sides
2 tablespoons confectioner's sugar
1/4 cup whipped cream

Serves 4
Preparation time 10 minutes, plus
   cooling time
Cooking time 26–28 minutes

1 Preheat the oven to 350°F. Place the blanched almonds in a colander and sprinkle with a little cold water. Shake off any excess water and place the almonds on a nonstick cookie sheet. Sift the confectioner's sugar over the top and bake for about 20 minutes until crystallized. Allow the almonds to cool, then put them in a freezer bag and tap lightly with a rolling pin until they are crushed but not powdery.

2 Mix together the grated chocolate, dates, and sliced almonds, and divide among 4 slices of the buttered brioche. Top with the remaining slices of brioche, to make a sandwich.

3 Heat a grill pan over a medium heat and place the brioche sandwiches on the grill for 3–4 minutes, then turn them over and toast the other side for another 3–4 minutes to create a panini.

4 Cut the panini in half diagonally and serve immediately with whipped cream and sprinkled with crushed almonds.

grilled pears with chocolate sauce

4 pears
1/4 cup sliced almonds, toasted
whipped cream or ice cream, to serve

Chocolate sauce
6 oz good-quality semisweet
   chocolate, with 70 percent cocoa
   solids
3 tablespoons water
1 tablespoon maple syrup
1 tablespoon butter

Serves 4
Preparation time 10 minutes
Cooking time 10 minutes

1 To make the chocolate sauce, half-fill a small saucepan with water, then fit an oven-proof bowl into the saucepan so that the bottom of the bowl is just immersed in the water. Bring the water to a gentle simmer. Put the chocolate, water, syrup, and butter into the bowl, allow to melt, then mix until the sauce is glossy and smooth.

2 Heat a grill pan over a medium heat. Peel the pears, if you like, then cut them into quarters and core. Place on the grill pan and cook for 2–3 minutes on each side.

3 Serve the grilled pears drizzled with the hot chocolate sauce and sprinkled with sliced almonds. To make this a really sensational dessert, serve it with whipped cream or a scoop of ice cream.

pancake stack with maple syrup

1 egg
2/3 cup unbleached all-purpose flour
1/2 cup milk
2 1/2 tablespoons vegetable oil
1 tablespoon sugar
8 scoops of vanilla ice cream
bottled maple syrup, to serve

Serves 4
Preparation time 10 minutes
Cooking time 6 minutes

1 To make the pancake batter, put the egg, flour, milk, oil, and sugar into a food processor and blend until smooth and creamy.

2 Heat a grill pan over a medium heat and place a ladleful of the batter in each corner, to make 4 pancakes.

3 After about 1 minute, the tops of the pancakes will start to set and air bubbles will rise to the top and burst. Using a spatula, turn the pancakes over and cook on the other side for 1 minute.

4 Repeat twice more until you have used all the batter—making 12 small pancakes in all. Bring to the table as a stack, drizzled with maple syrup. Serve 3 pancakes to each person, with scoops of ice cream.

drunken orange slices

4 large sweet oranges
1/4 cup cold water
1/4 cup brown sugar
3 tablespoons Cointreau
2 tablespoons whiskey
juice of 1 small orange
1 vanilla bean, split
1 cinnamon stick
4 cloves
2–3 mace blades (optional)
ginger ice cream, to serve

Serves 4
Preparation time 10 minutes
Cooking time 12 minutes

1 Using a small, sharp knife, cut off the base and the top of the oranges. Now cut down around the curve of the orange to remove all the peel and pith, leaving just the orange flesh. Cut the flesh horizontally into 1/4-inch slices and set aside.

2 In a small pan, very gently heat the water, sugar, 2 tablespoons of the Cointreau, the whiskey, orange juice, vanilla bean, cinnamon stick, cloves, and mace until the sugar has dissolved. Now turn up the heat and boil rapidly for 5 minutes. Cool slightly, but keep warm.

3 Heat a grill pan over a high heat, then quickly grill the orange slices for 1 minute on each side until caramelized. Top with the remaining Cointreau and set alight. Once the flames have died down, arrange the orange slices on serving dishes and drizzle with the flamed syrup.

4 Serve the orange slices immediately with the ginger ice cream, or an ice cream of your choice.

figs with yogurt and honey

8 ripe figs
4 tablespoons plain yogurt
2 tablespoons honey

Serves 4
Preparation time 5 minutes
Cooking time 10 minutes

Warm figs with plain yogurt and honey drizzled over the top make a delicious and quick dessert. Buy figs when they are in season and full of flavor and juice.

1 Heat a grill pan over a medium heat and add the figs. Cook for 8 minutes, turning occasionally, until they are charred on the outside. Remove and cut in half.

2 Arrange the figs on 4 plates and serve with a spoonful of plain yogurt and some honey spooned over the top.

grilled pineapple with rum and mascarpone

1 pineapple, peeled, cored, and cut into 8 slices
6 tablespoons mascarpone cheese (Italian cream cheese available at many supermarkets)
2 tablespoons rum
2 tablespoons fine brown sugar

Serves 4
Preparation time 5 minutes
Cooking time 5 minutes

1 Heat a grill pan over a medium heat. Put the pineapple slices on the grill and cook for 2 minutes on each side.

2 Mix together the mascarpone cheese, rum, and brown sugar. Serve the grilled pineapple with the mascarpone mixture spooned on top.

index

acknowledgements

Recipe Contributor: Jo Mcauley
Food Stylist: Joss Herd
Photography: Gareth Sambidge

Cookware generously provided by
All-Clad, Calphalon and Le Creuset.